SKINWALKERS

There are many different views on what a skin walker is. There are many different things you can find on the internet. Many cultures all over the world have their own myths and legends which have been passed through many generations. There are many different parts of the United States that have their version of the Skinwalker, but possibly the scariest of them all is the legend of the skinwalkers, most often attributed to the Navajo people. The best place to begin is the simple question as;

What is a skinwalker?

Here is a simple question but you get different answers to this question.

1. In Navajo (Navajo: Diné) culture, a skin-walker (yee naaldlooshii) is a type of witch who has the ability to turn into an animal, or to disguise themselves as an animal. (1)

2. A skinwalker is a person with the ability to turn into any animal they desire. The Navajo skinwalker is known as 'yee naaldlooshii' and is a variety of Navajo witch. It is apparently far more common for men to be skinwalkers, though it is possible for women as well. (2)

So really all we know is the Skinwalker is from the Native American mythology. If we really look at both definitions we can see that a skinwalker can be a witch of sort. We can also see that they turn themselves in animals of their desire. WE know that they are both male and female as well.

In looking for different things on skinwalkers online I found one site that did in fact give good information about them. I am going to share what was said on the site. (3) Young, B. (2016). *L. Tom Perry special collections.* Retrieved July 7, 2016, from

Skin-walkers are not boogiemen. They aren't figures made up to scare children. Unlike Anglo stories of werewolves and witches, they don't lose control and kill everything in their path or maliciously curse people for no reason. Like humans, they do kill, and like humans, they have motivations for those acts of aggression. Power and revenge fuel their murderous intent, but such things cannot occupy the brain of a rational creature all the time, and skin-walkers don't make murder part of their daily routine.

The most fantastic stories of skin-walkers are their origin stories. Non-skin-walkers are not allowed to view the rituals of becoming a skin-walker, so the creation of such creatures is the most shrouded in mystery of all their activities. The stories say that they must kill someone of close kin to become a skin-walker, but very little evidence exists to actually support this. Some say it must just be a kill, and that the person doesn't matter, but once again, these are the stories of those who are not invited to know anything about the initiation process and must be treated as such.

Other than their origin story, legends of skin-walkers rarely include death or even any kind of mauling. Common stories include skin-walkers in their animal form running alongside vehicles and matching their speeds whenever the driver attempts to accelerate. (FA 03 2.5.1.1.1) Eventually, they'll get bored of this game of chase and simply disappear into the surrounding wilderness. While this leaves the drivers unsettled, it is hardly enough to even label as malicious. Rather, it seems playful, like the small dog that chases after cars that pass on the street.

More malicious but tellingly less common, are the stories of skin-walkers stalking outside the dwellings of people who are home alone. Still, they never come in, despite the fact that Navajo hogans have a hole in the top, simplifying uninvited entry. Still, the result is unsettling rather than life-ending.

The fact that there aren't many stories of skin-walkers using their power to harm doesn't mean there aren't a few. The important thing to remember about skin-walkers is that they are human. Humans have created every great atrocity in history; for power or revenge, humans will go to great lengths. Skin-walkers have the ability to make sympathetic curses with the hair or clothing of their victims. Tradition dictates that Navajo people neither sweep nor comb their hair late at night when it could be captured by a skin-walker and used in a curse against them. (FA 01 400)

In the few stories that outsiders have heard of the effects of curses, they usually don't appear to be fatal. Slow onset pain or hallucinations appear to be the extent of the curse, and visiting a medicine man always solves the problem. (FA 01 271) Once, when a friend of a skin-walker felt wronged by her stepmother, she asked for a curse to be put on her, which caused her to experience voices until a priest came and exorcised the spirit haunting her at the skin-walker's behest. (FA 01 400) In each of the tales, the person deserved to have something happen to them, if not something so severe as a curse, but they were never left cursed to the point of death.

While it is possible that there are stories that are simply never told to outsiders that give cause to the blanket silence of those who make their home on reservations, it is also possible that they just don't like to talk about their neighbors when they can never know which one likes to run around at night in a predator's skin. Either way, the behavior of both the skin-walkers themselves as well as the people who live near them indicate that skin-walkers are not a story to scare children or even a warning to stay inside at night. They are real, and they are human, with all the benevolence and malevolence that comes with it.

Examples of Skin-walkers in the Special Collections Archives

Yenaalglooshii: Mormon Missionary Accounts of Werewolfism on the Navajo Indian Reservation (FA 01 271)

Many missionaries have experienced a skin-walker or 'yee naaldlooshii' running alongside their truck at night. They've also been in trailers when skin-walkers attempted to break in. Older missionaries will occasionally pretend to be skin-walkers to tease 'greenie' missionaries, so any tales of terrorized trailers should be filtered through a lens of hazing.

The legend that skin-walkers must kill for their power comes from people like one man who claimed to be an ex-apprentice who refused to perform the initiation rite. However, for every one story of a skin-walker killing someone, there are five more stories of a normal human shooting a skin-walker in their predator form and finding a neighbor dead or injured the next morning.

The Legends of the Wolfmen (FA 01 389)

One of the most poignant stories includes a young boy who followed his grandmother to the cave where she was performing skin-walker rituals. He got caught by another skin-walker and given the choice to join them or die for spying. Somehow, despite the fact that skin-walkers can run as fast as a car, the young boy was able to get away. He never saw his grandmother again.

From Werewolf to Hogan: The Navajo Experience as Seen Through a White Perspective (FA 01 400)

Dogs can always tell if a skin-walker is about. If a person who is being stalked by an angry skin-walker has dogs, the dogs will bark whenever the skin-walker gets near the hogan. Many skin-walkers look like dogs in their predator forms, but they run differently. Their gate has been described as the sideways gate of a great dog that has human legs folded up inside it.

This is one of the few places that gave really good information on skinwalkers. I have been researching them for a while now and trying to gather as much information as I can on them. The reason is I have come across a few of them and have had to deal with them. This whole book is to help people get a better reality of skinwalkers. It is also made to help people understand that skinwalkers are not fake; they are not to be taken likely. They are indeed dangerous.

On another site: (2) Faherty, A. (2015, May 7). Are you brave enough to read these terrifying stories about the Navajo skinwalkers? Retrieved July 7, 2016, from http://moviepilot.com/posts/2907100. This author has given a few things that are good as well. They say; Skinwalkers are most frequently seen as coyotes, wolves, foxes, eagles, owls or crows and are not creatures to be trusted. Some Navajo believe that skinwalkers have the ability to steal the face of a person, and some believe that if you ever lock eyes with a skinwalker they can absorb themselves into your body, or that your body might freeze up with fear, allowing a skinwalker to channel that fear to gain power and energy. There are many other horror stories about things that skinwalkers do to their victims, such as using a poison powder of corpse dust made from ground infant bones (preferably the finger and skull bones of twin infants) to kill them with.

Many cultures all over the world have their own myths and legends which have been passed through many generations. The Maori people of New Zealand have Taniwha, the Algonquian people of North America have Wendigo, but possibly the scariest of them all is the legend of the skinwalkers, most often attributed to the Navajo people.

What is a skinwalker?

A skinwalker is a person with the ability to turn into any animal they desire. The Navajo skinwalker is known as 'yee naaldlooshii' and is a variety of Navajo witch. It is apparently far more common for men to be skinwalkers, though it is possible for women as well.

Skinwalkers are most frequently seen as coyotes, wolves, foxes, eagles, owls or crows and are not creatures to be trusted. Some Navajo believe that skinwalkers have the ability to steal the face of a person, and some believe that if you ever lock eyes with a skinwalker they can absorb themselves into your body, or that your body might freeze up with fear, allowing a skinwalker to channel that fear to gain power and energy. There are many other horror stories about things that skinwalkers do to their victims, such as using a poison powder of corpse dust made from ground infant bones (preferably the finger and skull bones of twin infants) to kill them with.

Skinwalkers are a very intense legend, and while non-believers are quick to devise it as nothing but nonsense, many Navajo will share their chilling skinwalker stories.

Have people have real experiences with skinwalkers?

This is a question that has come to surface. Yes people have indeed came across them and had experiences with them. I am going to share you some and you can see what they went through.

1. A series of haunting events(2)

My uncle and cousin saw a large deer on the side of the road. When they got closer it hopped over the fence like a bipedal man. One time driving back from Gallup, my dad saw an old Navajo woman walking on the side of the road and when he slowed to offer her a ride she took off into the plains, quickly with inhuman speed. Once when I was a kid, my family was at my Aunt's house which is in a rural secluded area when we were toyed with by a few entities. They would make animal noises and when we looked to the direction from which the noises were coming they would turn a flashlight on and off. The noises would come from all directions, in increasingly shorter succession. Usually when I'm there, on the reservation visiting, alone late at night I will feel the presence of evil and dread, panic and paranoia will wash over me and as sudden as it comes it will leave.

Share by Redditor 6thgradehoodrat

2. Spooked cows and bipedal dogs

My family owns a farm in the heart of an Indian reservation. One winter I was home for Christmas taking care of the farm whiles my parents was away Christmas shopping. As I was home by myself, way late in the night and I hear all our cows freaking out. I knew it had to be the wild dogs that are rampant in the area. So I throw on some boots, grab a shotgun, load it up, and head out to the field. This was a perfect scenario for a horror movie, it was cloudy but there was full moon, and it was breaking through the clouds just right to light up all the snow. I ran out into the middle of the field, and just in time I see two dogs, they were standing up facing each other and fighting. I think "perfect two for one." So I pump a shell into the chamber of Mr. 12 gauge and then it happened. The two dogs heard the rack, they both stopped, looked over at me, and ran away, ON THEIR BACK LEGS. Immediately I froze, and every ghost story about

Skinwalkers and all the other Native legends I grew up with flew through my mind. Keep in mind I am a white guy, and up until then, these were all just boogie man stories the Native kids like to tell to scare us. That night, they became real to me.

3. A family escaping a screaming nightmare

So, this was the VERY early 80's, and my Sister, who lived in Toronto, came down to visit our Parents for a weekend. She was staying at a friend's house, who loaned her a car so she could come out. After her visit, she left a little after 9 pm. She got maybe 7-8 miles away when the car broke down. Thankfully, she broke down in front of a friend of the family's house. They let her in to call Dad, and Dad came to get her. The family said she could leave the car in their driveway for the night, and my Sister decided to just stay at my parents for the night. It was now a little after 10 pm and pitches black (Late November), while my Sister and Dad are driving back to the house and they pass through a heavily wooded area. Out of nowhere they hear this INCREDIBLY FUCKING LOUD inhuman SCREAM that was heard over the engine, them talking and the radio. Dad SLAMMED on the brakes and they both started freaking out, when suddenly a 6 foot tall Coyote walking on TWO LEGS with a black/white stripped tail appeared on the side of the road and proceeded to walk in front of the car. As soon as it passed, that same scream played again only this time 10x louder. Dad SLAMMED on the accelerator and they got the fuck out of there.

It was never seen again.

4. A bus trip goes sinister

...When we had crossed the rez's [reservations] border I noticed the bus driver had sped up and was now going about 85 mph. I thought this was a little weird because he never exceeded the speed limit, at least not in my high school career. For some reason, I couldn't fall asleep like the rest of my teammates, and I just sat at the back of the bus staring out across the desolate desert landscape that was lit up by the full moon. As I looked out, I could see a figure running towards the bus at an angle of pursuit...and keeping up with the bus at 85 mph. As the figure got closer I saw that it was a humanoid form. As a matter of fact it looked exactly like a human, only that the face was painted half black and half white with glowing eyes. Glowing eyes like a rabbit's eyes reflecting light from a spotlight. I immediately thought, "Holy crap! It's a skinwalker!!" The skinwalker ran up to the edge of the road and just kept up pace with the bus hurdling sage brush and rocks while staring at me. After I made eye contact with the thing, I COULD NOT looks away. It was as if something was holding my head and eyes in place. The skinwalker just smiled at me this inhuman smile that went ear-to-ear, showing crooked, yellow, pointed teeth. I felt like I was going to throw up and I was panicking through the whole ordeal. The skinwalker started to crumple down on to all fours, still keeping up with the bus. I could see his bones crack and reform, hair started appearing all over the skinwalker's body and in about 3 seconds was now a coyote and it ran off back into the desert out of view. As soon as it was gone, I ran to the onboard bathroom and puked a mixture of food and blood. I didn't want to tell anyone for fear they would think I was crazy. I confided in my Navajo friend. She told me that I needed to see the chief, who also happened to be a friend of mine, and get a blessing. I saw him the next school day in the parking lot. He just came up to me and mumbled something in Navajo while waving a feathered scepter-like thing, turned around, got in his truck and drove away. To this day, I haven't seen another skinwalker.

5. The rocking dog

Not me but my uncle. He is Mexican/Native American. This happened in the Mojave Desert in southern California. He was driving around with his girlfriend late at night and they saw something that looked like a huge black dog on the side of the road. He slowed down and the dog began crossing the road. Instead of walking like a normal dog would, this thing moved like a toy rocking horse. He said it stopped in the middle of the road and stared right at them and its eyes had a red glow. My uncle is the most badass person I know and it scared the crap out of him.

6. YENALDLOOSHI IS WATCHING ME (4)

My grandmother on my mother's side has always been very Superstitious, for lack of better word, she's not religious, but she does believe in a lot of paranormal stuff. Her mother was full-blooded Navajo and her father was Irish. Either way, she'd never been anywhere east of Montana or she grew up in Nevada. One year, when I was in grade school, we went to visit her, most of the visit was pretty uneventful, typical boring old people stuff, except she always kept her curtains drawn shut and would always peek out the window and when someone asked what she was doing, she would simply reply " Yenaldlooshi is watching me"

This went on for nearly the entire visit until a few days before we were due to leave, My grandma and my (then) baby brother (he's 19 now lol) were in the front yard that evening, planting flowers when all of a sudden, my grandmother starts shouting "Insert little brothers name here get away from that creature! It's not safe!" of course, being in Nevada, we all assumed that my brother had found a scorpion or a rattle snake, so we all run outside, to see my Grandmother clutching my little brother and shaking in terror against the side of the house, standing out in the yard, was a large, black, great-dane sized dog, it was staring at my grandmother with an intensity I'd never seen before. It looked up at us, gave a little huff and bounded off, I don't remember if it moved unusually fast or not, but do remember it had really deep yellow eyes. When my mother asked my grandmother what had happened, she kept repeating" The Yenaldlooshi has found me". She moved a couple weeks after that.

7. ON THE REZ ALONE AT NIGHT

My uncle and cousin saw a large deer on the side of the road. When they got closer it hopped over the fence like a bipedal man. One time driving back from Gallup, my dad saw an old Navajo woman walking on the side of the road and when he slowed to offer her a ride she took off into the plains, quickly with inhuman speed. Once when I was a kid, my family was at my Aunt's house which is in a rural secluded area when we were toyed with by a few entities. They would make animal noises and when we looked to the direction from which the noises were coming they would turn a flashlight on and off. The noises would come from all directions, in increasingly shorter succession. Usually when I'm there, on the reservation visiting, alone late at night I will feel the presence of evil and dread, panic and paranoia will wash over me and as sudden as it comes it will leave.

8. IT MOVED LIKE A TOY ROCKING HORSE

My uncle is Mexican and Native American. This happened in the Mojave Desert in southern California. He was driving around with his girlfriend late at night and they saw something that looked like a huge black dog on the side of the road. He slowed down and the dog began crossing the road. Instead of walking like a normal dog would, this thing moved like a toy rocking horse. He said it stopped in the middle of the road and stared right at them and its eyes had a red glow. My uncle is the most badass person I know and it scared the crap out of him.

9. THEY RAN AWAY ON THEIR BACK LEGS

So this happened about twelve years ago. My family owns a farm in the heart of an Indian reservation. One Winter I was home for Christmas taking care of the farm whiles my parents was away Christmas shopping. As I was home by myself, way late in the night and I hear all our cows freaking out. I knew it had to be the wild dogs that are rampant in the area. So I throw on some boots, grab a shotgun, load it up, and head out to the field. This was a perfect scenario for a horror movie, it was cloudy but there was full moon, and it was breaking through the clouds just right to light up all the snow.

I ran out into the middle of the field, and just in time I see two dogs, they were standing up facing each other and fighting. I think "perfect two for one." So I pump a shell into the chamber of Mr. 12 gauge and then it happened. The two dogs heard the rack; they stopped, looked over at me, and ran away, ON THEIR BACK LEGS. Immediately I froze, and every ghost story about Skinwalkers and all the other Native legends I grew up with flew through my mind. Keep in mind I am a white guy, and up until then, these were all just boogie man stories the Native kids like to tell to scare us. That night, they became real to me.

10. IT HAD A DOG'S BODY BUT WITH HUMAN HANDS AND FEET

I was spending a month with my cousins at my grandma's house. It was August and my cousin's ages ranged from ten to fifteen, and I was the oldest (being fifteen). I was staying with a ten, thirteen, and fourteen year old. We stayed up telling scary stories often, but one night a few weeks in, we decided to make a campfire out back. My grandma's house is in a rural suburb, the neighbors aren't too far when you're driving down the road to her house, but in the backyard, it's thick forest with manmade paths through it. Each house is on a hill so only part of the basement was actually underground. That isn't important until later though. So, we're towards the east side of her yard, in a smallish patch of open land. You couldn't see the neighboring yards from there, and there was probably three quarters a mile to each side of us that belonged to my grandma.

It was maybe eleven at night, and we were playing truth or dare after telling scary stories, and my fourteen year old cousin dared me and the thirteen year old to go walk through the paths for ten minutes or so. I said yes right away, as I wasn't easily scared and rather level headed, but my younger cousin was a bit more hesitant. We didn't bring a flashlight because it wasn't pitching dark yet, and we could see enough to not die. We were walking through the paths for about five minutes and could barely see the fire through the trees when we decided to turn. In the middle of the path, was a large dog-like creature, hunched over with its front hands an inch from the ground.

What I remember most was how its eyes were so fucking bright white, and it was humanoid-dog shaped with a human like head but a dog like body but human hands and feet. It looked right at us and I know I was paralyzed with fear as it dashed away the opposite way from us, towards a creek that ran through the yard. Eventually my cousin and I screamed bloody effin murder and the other cousins and my grandma ran to us. I don't remember much here because I was really disoriented and I couldn't think properly, but I did wake up in bed, so I assume that I was brought up to the house. All the kids slept in the basement, in a big room with sliding glass doors to the outside, as the room was on the side that wasn't underground. My bed was pressed against a big glass window, and I could see my cousins playing outside down below. the house is in Michigan so it gets slightly chilly even in the end of August, and there was a slight breeze so I put on a jacket and ran to join them outside, skipping breakfast, not wanting to miss out on anything fun.

When I got down I could tell they weren't playing but rather running to get my grandma. Her dogs–both of them–were dead, ripped up. That night we went to bed early. I woke up at maybe two in the morning because I felt something hit my head. My cousins were all sitting on the double bed opposite me on the other side of the room. There was one bunk bed and two double beds, the double beds for me and my fourteen year old cousin. They were being quiet and staring at me. The thirteen year old nodded his head toward the window. I froze. They all looked afraid. I turned my head slightly to the side and I saw a really messed up looking face pressed to the window with gaping eyes looking down at me. I screamed so fucking loud, and it bolted. My grandma called the police after I told her what happened and they found nothing. I went home after that and I have never been there during the night again.

11. IT WAS NEITHER FULLY HUMAN NOR FULLY ANIMAL

In July 2004, near Gallup, New Mexico, I had my first and only encounter with a Skinwalker. Before this I use to say "I'll believe it when I see it." Well, I'm a believer now. What I saw was neither full human nor full animal. I was moving and had just completed the cleaning and was with my 10-year-old son. We had called it a night and were headed to our new place. As we walked out the front door, I saw a figure move from behind my neighbor's car to a nearby tree that stood between our apartments. It didn't have red glowing eyes, snarling teeth, or a rotten smell. It did move quickly, but not quick enough to avoid the light from a nearby light post and the porch lights. It didn't look at me or come toward me…. It moved as if trying to avoid being seen. I was within fifteen feet of it, but I did not look back to fully inspect it. What I saw was a wolf-like animal that sort of resembled the beast in "Beauty and the Beast" just not cartoonish. It had brown fur that completely covered it, it wasn't a pelt, and it was a very large wolf. It didn't have any human traits except that it walked on its hind legs. It cowered behind the tree as we got into our vehicle. When we got in, I asked my son, "did you see that??!" Thankfully, he hadn't. My brother-in-law insists that it wasn't a Skinwalker because I would have never seen it. To this day, I can picture what it looked like, know they exist, and pray I never encounter one again.

12. THE GROVE

This didn't happen to me but a very close friend of mine. I've heard a lot about coyotes and Skinwalkers, and had a weird experience or two with coyotes (creepiest was waking up to my sleeping bag being surrounded in paw prints without ever hearing them during the night) but never anything paranormal so to speak. Patrick's story, however, kept me from going back to a favorite backcountry secret stash. He was leaving the area one morning, had been camping there a couple days and said there was a coyote that always seemed to be close by, like in his peripheral vision but never overt. He loaded up his truck and started to drive down the wash out to the fire road. At the end of the wash, he could see the coyote following him. When he pulled onto the road, it was running next to him. Now he was freaked out, so he sped up. He said he was going 35 or so, and it was running along beside him. Definitely not possible. When he looked back, the coyote was running on two legs and was wearing what Patrick said looked like buckskin pants. An instant later, it was a person wearing a coyote fur keeping pace with his truck. When he looked again… It was gone.

We never went back to the grove after that.

13. IT WAS LIKE IT KNEW WE KNEW WHAT IT REALLY WAS

I decided to join my bestie Karen for a three day stay at her grandmother's place on the Rez. Her Grandmother lives near a Place called Tuba City, Arizona. In the middle of nowhere but surrounded by rural homes. We go to college together and I was kind of interested to know about Navajo tradition. The first day we stayed, it was pretty chill…nothing out of the ordinary but then her Grandma (Not that old, around 67) said that a stray dog came out of nowhere and wouldn't leave. To me…it did act kind of strange and ugly looking. (Black, shaggy coat, looked like a mix between a German Shepard and a Lab)

That night, we were watching a movie in the living-room (had big windows that looked out into the front where the cars are parked, nothing fancy) with the curtains wide open, Grandma was in the kitchen cooking dinner and we were watching a movie. Next to the window is a medium bookshelf and where DVD's are kept. Karen went to put back a DVD we had just watched, but she freaked out because that stray black dog was staring at us through the window standing on-top of the wood-box outside. Not something normal dogs do from my point of view or hers. (Usually my dog which is a house Dog, scratches the door to be let in…Rez Dogs aren't house Dogs and Dogs inside houses are frowned upon in Navajo Tradition; Meant to protect the house and owner.) The other dogs seemed to stay away from it. Karen opened the door and yelled at it to get it off the box. It ran off behind the shed. We went to to Tuba City to get some groceries, came back to the house. The dog was nowhere to be seen, nothing unusual. Grandma went to visit some people so it was just Karen and I. About 5 o'clock we heard someone trying to open the door; both of us looked out since there had been no car heard and no dogs barking. Looking out the living-room window to the door and there was the DOG trying to open the door with its paws. Two paws wrapped around the brass door knob, standing on its hind-legs.

I thought that was…weird but wasn't really freaked out, Karen was. She opened the door and chased it off. Grandma came back later and Karen told her, Grandma didn't like what she heard. Got ready to sleep, we slept in the spare bedroom since it had two beds. One window with curtains opened a little. We turned off the light, but there was a sound coming from on top of the roof. Pitter-patter footsteps and scratching sounds and panting. It then sounded like it jumped off onto the large plastic water barrel they had. At first we heard what sounded like barking, but as it grew louder, the other dogs seemed to be barking at something also. But all of a sudden, something was running around the house barking and it was no DOG…NOPE….it wasn't.

This barking sounded human, a deep male voice barking like it knew that 'we' knew it wasn't a dog.

"Wuuuuff…wuff…wuff…Ruffff….Rrrrrrruuufff……….Arffffff….Arff Arff." Just exactly like that, adding the W's, R's and A's. Then panting again by the window and we started freaking out.

Karen decided to (in my opinion was stupid) open the curtains to look out, there was the stray dog on its hind legs looking into our bedroom but this time, it stunk and what I thought were two black holes in the neck, another pair of eyes twinkled (think of those ugly glossy spider eyes staring at you) and the paws were deformed looking hands with over-grown somewhat thick and sharp fingernails. Again…both screaming and shutting the curtains closed, Grandma came running through the door and seeing it. First thing she did was grab ashes from the fireplace, load three shells into the shotgun from under her bed, bless herself in Navajo and went outside to shoot it. Yelling in Navajo about how the 'thing' wasn't welcomed there and to get the hell outta there, for it go to linger somewhere else. Them both being traditional, the next day they called a Medicine Man to come-over and put cedar in. He prayed over everyone with cedar smoke and an eagle feather, blessed the place…made us eat bitter herbs called 'Eagles Gull' or something and gave me an arrowhead. Apparently I needed to carry one for protection and a little pouch called Corn-pollen. Seems to work pretty well.

The Medicine Man said that dog was a Skinwalker (Which in Navajo is a long word but I call them Yoshi's), the body of the stray dog (Which was killed by the Skinwalker) made an illusion so we wouldn't know it wasn't a real dog. He also said that Yoshi's tend to harm people by using some sort of human bone straw to spit at someone (think…spitballs only deadlier) and get human bones into them. Doctors can't detect it, but the Medicine Man that day pulled a piece of human skull out of Grandmas right shoulder, pretty big…about 2 inches long and 1 cm thick…it was real because we watched him pull it out of her…that was intense.

Now in all these accounts, some people are still skeptical on them. Some may say that they are fake and people were just scared. Yet people do not believe the unknown. They want to believe that there are not things out there that they cannot explain. Skinwalkers are real; there are too many accounts to just blow this off.

Rocky Mountain Legends

(5) They are accounts of nighttime drives on the lonely road between Farmington, NM and The Four Corners when, in the distance ahead, a coyote appears on the roadway, its eyes glowing in the headlights. Except that they are not coyote eyes, they are something else, something almost human, and when the car speeds past the waiting coyote the coyote bolts and begins speeding along with it, running at 60 miles per hour, its eyes still aglow in the headlights. The driver looks away and presses pedal to metal, and when he looks back suddenly it is no longer a coyote running at pace next to the vehicle, but a man. A man with the yellow eyes of a coyote fixed on the driver, one hand banging on the hood.

Or another story from the desert town of Tuba City, Arizona near Monument Valley, where a building contractor is doing repairs on an old ranch home. Thinking himself alone, the man is surprised to hear laughter coming from somewhere off in the sheep pens. Following the noise, the man turns a corner to the edge of the sheep pen where before him the entire flock is huddled shivering into one end of the pen while on the other a lone ram stands separated. He is standing upright, his two front hooves across his chest and his horned head thrown back in gleeful, maniacal laughter that is unmistakably human. Watching this, the man jumps and suddenly the ram spots him. For a fleeting moment the two lock eyes and, just like the laughter, the ram's eyes are familiar and anything but animal. The ram falls back down to all fours and mills along as if nothing had ever happened.

They are stories of shape-shifting creatures acrosss Navajo Nation, the 24k-plus reservation land encompassing most of northeastern Arizona and the adjacent corner sections of New Mexico and Utah. A taboo subject amongst natives, Skinwalkers are seldom discussed with members outside the tribe, and rarely even inside it. The Navajo Skinwalker legend is not unlike that of the European werewolf: A once-ordinary human discovers the ability to shift into animal form at night where his doings then become almost exclusively evil. Unlike the werewolf, however, the Skinwalker curse is desired and acquired, that is, Skinwalkers do not have the bad luck to be "bitten" and forced into the curse. Rather, they want it and are willing to perform extraordinary rites of evil in order to achieve it.

There are multiple legends behind the origin of the Navajo Skinwalker. One claims the Navajos mastered shapeshifting in order to escape persecution and relocation — the Kit Carson-led cornering of the tribe deep in Canyon de Chelly and later their forced and disastrous relocation to Bosque de Redondo. Another version relates to the Navajo belief in the Anasazi curse — that the Anasazi were responsible for the prevailing witchcraft in the Navajo tribes — and that Navajo Skinwalkers used the off-limit Anasazi ruins and grave sites to gain certain powers.

The most prominent history of the Skinwalker tells of a particular form of Navajo witch, or an 'ánt'įįhnii, called ayee naaldlooshii, translated to mean "with it, he goes on all fours." The yee naaldlooshii is usually a medicine man or high-ranking priest who has obtained supernatural powers through breaking a cultural taboo, including murder, seduction, or the corrupting of a family member.

Upon accepting this deep and consuming level of witchcraft, Skinwalkers are banished forever from a tribe (but considering the foreknowledge of this as well the despicable acts required for the transformation, the aspiring Skinwalker surely possessed an early, pre-seated hate for the tribe). Prowling alone in the desert, a Skinwalker (and also unlike the werewolf) has the ability to shape-shift into any animal they wish, although most commonly the animal is a coyote, wolf, cougar, fox, owl, or crow — a reason why pelts of these animals are widely restricted among the Navajo.

In animal form the eyes of a Skinwalker are distinctly human, while in human form this is reversed. Varying versions of the legend attribute Skinwalkers the ability to "body-snatch", to take possession of another person's body if that person locks eyes long enough with the Skinwalker. It is also said Skinwalkers, through this same eye-locking method, have the power to read human thoughts or even mimic perfectly the voice of that person, a ploy used to lure relatives. Skinwalkers are also said to use voodoo-like tactics to manipulate their victims, such as collecting a target's hair, wrapping it around a pottery shard, then burying it in a tarantula hole.

Outcasts and pariahs, Skinwalkers assume begrudged and hate-driven existences, their spirits in constant search of revenge or else mindless harm. The more modest accounts of Skinwalker encounters portray them as mischievous, almost poltergeist-like. They will climb the roofs of sleeping families, bang on the walls and knock on the windows. More commonly though, Skinwalkers stories are far more malicious. In these accounts Skinwalkers climb roofs in order to seek ways into the house and attack the family, or else they assault cars driving through reservation land, causing wrecks.

They are described as fast and agile, ugly mutations that are not quite human and not fully animal. Usually they are naked but some sightings report a creature wearing tattered shirts or jeans. In some stories the Skinwalker is actually tracked down only to lead to the home of a relative of the tracker. Or, like the werewolf, the Skinwalker will be shot and the next day a Navajo will be found with the same exact wound, revealing him as the ánt'įįhnii. Certain Navajo myths insist that the only way to fully kill a Skinwalker is with a bullet dipped in white ash.

So the next question everyone wants to know is;

How to kill a skinwalker?

(6) According to Navajo legend, the Skinwalker has the power to read human thoughts, allowing it to use the victim's own fears and secrets against them. The Skinwalker has the ability to control the minds of its victims, forcing them to comply with whatever the Skinwalker may have in mind. The Skinwalker is also able to mimic any human or animal sounds it chooses, perhaps using the voice of a loved one to lure a potential victim out of his or her home. It may also use this ability to distract homeowner so that it may steal property (like livestock) or to escape. The Skinwalker is adept in the use of black magic, using charms, chants, and spells to induce supernatural fear into its chosen victims, so that it may manipulate them into doing the Skinwalker's bidding. It may use this ability to induce fear to curse its victims or even to kill them. It is possible that the Skinwalker's very presence induces supernatural fear into both people and animals. The Skinwalker has a wide variety of weapons at its disposal, in addition to the human shinbone bows and arrows mentioned earlier. One of the most potent of these is a tiny bone pellet, which is fired from a blowgun into a victim's body. These pellets imbed themselves into the skin without leaving so much as a mark, and afterwards causes sickness, social misfortune, and eventual death. Bone dust, once again made from ground-up infant bones, induces bodily paralysis and eventual heart failure. Another spell that the Skinwalker uses to kill is done by acquiring some of its victim's hair, wrapping it around a potshard, and placing it into a tarantula's hole. Live rattlesnakes may be released into the victim's dwelling or his bed, causing him to grow sick and die from the rattlesnake's bite. The Skinwalker also loves to cause trouble between the world of the living and the realm of the dead. The Skinwalker digs

up a corpse, severs a finger or another small body part, and hides it inside the home of the intended victim. The ghost of the deceased will rise from the grave in search of its missing body part, and will then haunt whoever possesses it. The home's owners will be both confused and terrified as to why this is happening to them.

The Skinwalker is notoriously hard to kill, and defeating one requires the assistance of a powerful shaman, who knows spells and rituals that can turn the Skinwalker's evil back upon itself. These medicine men charge an exorbitant fee for their services, but most victims are more than willing to pay after being unduly harassed by the Skinwalker. As for more mundane means, attempting to shoot or otherwise kill one of these creatures is usually unsuccessful, as the Skinwalker can use its magic to make guns jam, and can even stop the bullets in mid-air. Even if the bullets do hit the Skinwalker, they may not have any effect whatsoever. However, if the creature actually is wounded by chance and manages to escape, a similar wound will appear on the Skinwalker's human form. In the Werewolf folklore of Europe, this phenomenon is known as sympathetic wounding. This leaves the creature clearly marked and makes it vulnerable to discovery, and will be dealt with according to tradition. If one knows who the Skinwalker truly is, he must say "(name of the accused), you are a Skinwalker." The witch will fall sick and die within three days time. Similarly, if a Skinwalker is captured and the news is broadcast, the witch will die within a year.

The only way to kill a Skinwalker, according to Navajo legend, is to shoot the creature with bullets that have been dipped into white ash (although some legends say that silver will work as well). Even then, the Skinwalker must be shot through the neck while the witch is in animal form. The bullet will strike the Skinwalker's real head, and any shot that is aimed elsewhere will pass harmlessly through the body. It is said that, if wounded, the Skinwalker will bleed a yellow liquid instead of blood. However, there is a way to defeat the Skinwalker without actually killing the creature, although if the attempt is successful, it will surely prompt the witch's revenge. The Skinwalker is able to speak while in animal form, but it will not willingly do so because it may cause the witch to permanently lose his powers. If one could trick the creature into speaking while in animal form, it will reassume its human form and will be unable to shapeshift ever again.

It is said that sometimes the Skinwalker is invisible to human eyes, but it will leave tracks that are larger than those of any natural beast. It's very bad luck to cross over a Skinwalker's tracks if the creature is in front of them – one must step over them. As well as the creature's eyes, the Skinwalker can be distinguished from a real animal in that its tail hangs down and moves constantly, while their ears move up and down constantly as well. The Skinwalker's eyes, as well as glowing when the creature is in human form and vice-versa in animal form, are seen as mere slits in their masks. Against the Skinwalker's poison, the gall of an eagle, a bear, or a mountain lion are the best remedies. Sweats will help rid oneself of the fear of Skinwalkers.

There are many different ways online that will tell you how to kill a skinwalker. There is shooting them with a bullet of silver, or a bullet that is double dipped in white ash. There is also to call out the skinwalkers name. it really is hard to say as to per say that will kill a skinwalker. There is no facts that say "This is how you kill one".

So now the next question that others are asking is;

How to deal with a skinwalker?

First it is how do you know one is close by? That is something you need to know before you know how to deal with one.

- Presence makes you feel like something bad is around.

"Then out of nowhere I just felt this dark feeling of fear and dread. I had no idea why I was feeling this way but I definitely felt that something was wrong."

- Animal like:

"dark silhouette of something very tall and very skinny that seemed to be covered with some kind of hair or fur running behind the truck after us! Whatever it was, it wasn't a normal human or human at all"

They practice:

"about black magic, witches, and something that the Navajos call Yee Nadlooshii or Skinwalkers"

smell bad & their presence makes you feel something evil is around.

"We knew they were skin walkers because you could smell dead animals and feel something evil was around you."

- Putting ash around is a protective mechanism. Is this just for skinwalkers or does this have deeper meaning of protection against evil?

"I put ash around the tents because I wanted to be protected"

- They have an appearance of being animal like.

"What freaked us out the most was we saw what looked like goats feet and horns like a deer walk in front of the fire where we saw it clearly."

Other than that there is; Do not look a Skinwalker in the eyes, for to do so will put you under their power and allow them to possess you. Pay attention to animals. Animals will act extremely bizarre when a Skinwalker is around as they can sense it's presence. Also, animals that a Skinwalker transforms into can hurt it when it is in such animal form. For example, if a Skinwalker is in Coyote form then another Coyote could attack it for stealing the shape of it's kind and mimicking their spirit, as the Skinwalker is an impostor. Be observant. When a Skinwalker transforms it never fully imitates perfectly an animal. There will always be something "off" or "not right" about it. For example, a Skinwalker may be too large in animal form or may walk strangely. Skinwalkers usually do not physically attack their victims upon the first meeting. Instead, they like to steal hair or fingernail clippings to use in black magic against the person first. So make sure to properly dispose of such items so that a Skinwalker cannot get them. Skinwakers can be killed with bullets or other weapons that have been blessed by a medicine man and dressed with holy ash.

Now for me I will tell you what I know how to deal with a skinwalker.

1. You have to understand them
2. You cannot show fear, they feed off it
3. You need to make a dream catcher and put them around your home (one made of earth. Example: tree branches, yarn, feathers and beads)
4. You need to try to keep your mind blank when you see them. They can read your mind. You do not want them to use things against you.
5. You need to figure out their true name. This helps keep them at bay and keep them away. They do not want others to know who they are so knowing that name will make you have some power over them
6. Keep your charm with you. This is where you keep what makes you feel safe and protected.
7. Make sure you have some sort of barrier around you. Salt works wonders
8. Show them they have no power over you. Show them you are more powerful than them.

Now I am not telling people to go stand up to a skinwalker. I would not advice it. I would however advice to keep away from them. You really do not want to mess with them. Skenwalkers need to be take them seriously. If you do not understand them or know much about them do not try to take one on. You should really find someone that has knowledge about them to really deal with them.

Now the only things I can find that will help you know there is a skinwalker around is the normal; Prints of animal to human prints, The sounds of animal and human noises together, and the smell.

There are a few things online that have gave this information as well. Here is one that I found that was pretty good.

(7) 1) Skinwalkers can take any mammal form large enough to get ahold of. (Mostly Dogs, Sheep, Foxes, Horses, Deer, Cows, Coyote, Sometimes a Wolf or Cougar pelt but Wolves aren't seen much around Navajo Land. And Cougars are to territorial and vicious for them to kill. Bobcats...are usually left out.) It depends on what they want and why.

2) They smell awful. (Dead Fish, Roadkill, Something Rotting.)

3) When in human form they wear alot of Navajo traditional jewelry (Dug up from Navajo Graves and stolen) and they tend to wear an over amount of it (3 Turquoise bracelets, 4 or 5 necklaces of different Navajo necklaces, a vast amount of turquoise rings when in Yoshi mode.)

4) The reason they smell horrid is to let the living know what they are and also to make a person faint from smell.

5) They can also make a person (If caught up in terror upon seeing them) act against their will much like Psychosis, Catatonia, Heart-attack, Stroke, Immobilized and Fainting.

6) Instead of using Sage to cleanse ones self, it is best to use Cedar/Juniper Smoke and Cedar ash against Entities.

7) Skinwalkers and Coyotes always go hand-in-hand and a Skinwalker never travels by itself.

8) Skinwalkers aren't spiritual, its frowned upon in Navajo Tradition. Its much like how people view Cannibalization on the living or dead and being a Skinwalker is like inviting a Demon to take over ones body.

9) Witchcraft is used by nearly all Yoshi's, called "The Bad Way," If one gets ahold of something of yours (a piece of clothing, hair, etc) they can use it against you. They also can put both animal bones or human bones into your body without you knowing it but usually it become apparent if you suddenly feel like you've got something sharp under your skin.

10) They can travel a vast distance within hours. Also some are suspected to be able to fly (But said Medicine Man doesn't think so.) If one is shot, it would be known if the Yoshi turns back into the person...example. ("Edison said he accidentally shot himself in the leg while hunting yesterday.")

11) Yoshi's can manipulate animals and insects: Snakes, Spiders, Coyotes, Dogs, Owls, Crows. (Ex: Imagine your going to some place and you've stopped...the Navajo guy in-front of you is taking to long to get gas, you cuss him out and he gives your a evil look then finishes. You get out of your car to get gas, after you get in. Ready to go back on the road. You hear what sounds like a rattle. Look down and there under the gas pedal is a Rattlesnake.)

12) Whistling at night apparently calls Skin-walkers and Demons. If one whistles back from the dark outta nowhere and you're by yourself out camping..there you have it, pat yourself on the back because you just succeeded in calling one. Now...the question in mind is how to get rid of it...goooood luck with that.

13) Making eye contact will cause you to loose control of your mind and body.

14) Skinwalkers also use paint (Red, Black, Grey and White) to cover their face and body.

15) They will harass the person or family at night and if bold...during the day. (Banging on doors, windows and running atop the roof.) Running after cars or posing as a hitch-hiker while on a lonely road at night. (Running after the car or truck, hitting the side of car, try to smash window in, jumping on car's roof or hood, etc)

16) Most Navajo's are hesitant to speak about their experience with Skinwalkers. (Some Skinwalkers are usually Neighbors or Relatives.) (Someone is always some-else's enemy sorta deal) But most keep it secret if they are a Yoshi. SO none of the family, friends or relations will know.

17) Reasons why people become Skinwalkers. (Passed from Family Member or Friend to do evil, Jealousy, Greed and the 7 deadly Sins to get what they want, Hate and Power.)

18) Skinwalkers tend to be Navajo and only Navajo unless another Tribe/Race speaks Navajo well and has connections. Usually the person who becomes a Skinwalker does so by being chanted over and also praying to Evil in 85-100% Navajo Language.

20) The Ceremony held is in secret, far away from prying eyes. Much like a VIP sorta deal and only the people who are invited will come. But most don't even know what kinda ceremonious event will take place until its to late. (Ex: In Canyon Walls or in deserted Hogans.) Many become this through a series of tests. (Ex: Digging up Graves, Eating the dead, Killing family members, Drinking Blood of Humans and Docile Animals, Practicing Witchcraft and alot more)

21) Gender don't matter as-well as age. (Female, Male, Children, Teens, Elders, Young Adults)

22) If you've seen one, you'll never be able to forget it and you'll lose sleep over it.

23) The Lifespan is the same as the life span of a normal human. There's no undead or remaining young forever kinda thing. Nor do they change into a Werewolf on the full moon. They can change anytime the want.

24) Its Taboo to drive though Navajo Land after 9:00 at night because you'll get lost and see things you wish you'd never seen.

25) Arrowheads one of the artifacts that protects you from a Yoshi (Unless is isn't Native Made then...Sucks to be you.)

26) The way of the Skinwalker is changing and becoming more horrific then it previously was do to the next generation's interest. (Ex: Long sharp needle like teeth, Black Scleras, Ability to Fly, etc)

I hope you understand the world of skinwalkers. This book is to help you understand them better. Thank you for allowing me to show you more about them and help you understand more about them. Skinwalkers are not to be taken lightly. They are out there. And they are dangerous.

References:

1. Skin-walker (2016). . In Wikipedia. Retrieved from https://en.wikipedia.org/wiki/Skin-walker

2. Faherty, A. (2015, May 7). Are you brave enough to read these terrifying stories about the Navajo skinwalkers? Retrieved July 7, 2016, from http://moviepilot.com/posts/2907100

3. Young, B. (2016). L. Tom Perry special collections. Retrieved July 7, 2016, from https://sites.lib.byu.edu/worldhistory/folklore-william-a-wilson-folklore-archives/popular-search-topics/skin-walkers-navajo-legend/

4. Sean. (2015, October 5). Sean. Retrieved July 7, 2016, from Bizarre, http://www.cvltnation.com/12-people-tell-their-terrifying-encounters-with-navajo-skinwalkers/

5. adamjamesjones. (2011, July 28). Skinwalkers. Retrieved July 7, 2016, from https://adamjamesjones.wordpress.com/2011/07/28/skinwalkers/

6. Swope, P., & profile, V. my complete. (2008). The paranormal pastor. Retrieved July 7, 2016, from http://theparanormalpastor.blogspot.com/2012/07/the-navajo-skinwalker.html

7. deleted. (2015, February 21). About Navajo Skinwalkers • /r/skinwalkers. Retrieved July 7, 2016, from https://www.reddit.com/r/skinwalkers/comments/2wlsw1/about_navajo_skinwalkers/

www.ingramcontent.com/pod-product-compliance
Lightning Source LLC
Chambersburg PA
CBHW050918290526
45792CB00002B/796